Along The Tavy

Chips Barber

All the very best!

Chips Barber

OBELISK PUBLICATIONS

Also by the Author

Diary of a Dartmoor Walker
Diary of a Devonshire Walker
Ten Family Walks on Dartmoor
Ten Family Walks in East Devon
Six Short Pub Walks on Dartmoor
The Great Little Dartmoor Book
The Great Little Chagford Book
Beautiful Dartmoor
Dark and Dastardly Dartmoor
Weird and Wonderful Dartmoor
Cranmere Pool – The First Dartmoor Letterbox
The Teign Valley of Yesteryear, Parts I and II
Princetown of Yesteryear, Parts I and II
Widecombe – A Visitor's Guide
Railways on and around Dartmoor
Around & About Tavistock
Around & About Roborough Down

Other Dartmoor Titles

The Great Walks of Dartmoor, *Terry Bound*
The A to Z of Dartmoor Tors, *Terry Bound*
Walks in the Chagford Countryside, *Terry Bound*
Walks in the Shadow of Dartmoor, *Denis McCallum*
Walks in Tamar and Tavy Country, *Denis McCallum*
The Templer Way, *Derek Beavis*
The Dartmoor Mountain Bike Guide, *Peter Barnes*
Circular Walks on Eastern Dartmoor, *Liz Jones*
Under Sail Through South Devon and Dartmoor, *Raymond B. Cattell*

We have over 150 Devon titles. For a full list of current books, please contact us at
Obelisk Publications, 2 Church Hill, Pinhoe, Exeter, Devon, EX4 9ER or telephone (01392) 468556.

Acknowledgements

All photographs by Chips Barber, drawing on page 7 by Jane Reynolds.

First published in 1998 by
Obelisk Publications, 2 Church Hill, Pinhoe, Exeter, Devon
Designed by Chips and Sally Barber
Typeset by Sally Barber
Printed in Great Britain by
The Devonshire Press Ltd, Torquay, Devon

Along The Tavy

The River Tavy rises on a peaty plateau in 'the middle of nowhere'. Or that is how some might describe the highly elevated wilderness which gives birth to one of Devon's fastest-flowing rivers. It is a river which begins on the heights of Northern Dartmoor to flow down to join the Tamar, at Bere Ferrers, passing through some wonderful countryside on its way. This book features just some of the stories of the people and places found along its banks and has been written as part of a trilogy. For those who want to know more about the ancient stannary town that it passes, *Around & About Tavistock* should also be read. For those who are curious about Buckland Abbey, Buckland Monachorum and the Yelverton district, *Around & About Roborough Down* should prove of interest.

The Tavy's origin is the subject of a local legend. Although clearly only a story, it's included here because, like most legends, it is based on reality.

Tamara was a beautiful troglodyte living deep in the bowels of the earth with her parents, who were committed cave dwellers. However, she yearned for the surface life of sunshine and breeze and so, whenever the opportunity arose, she crept out onto the surface. She danced about in the warmth of the sunlight, and caught the eye of two giants called Tavy and Torridge. Although they were good friends, they soon became rivals as they both fell hopelessly head-over-heels in love with this subterranean siren.

One day, after much pursuit, Tavy and Torridge cornered Tamara and asked her to choose between them, a 'giant' problem if ever there was one. Respecting both their feelings, Tamara found herself in a dilemma. But whilst she mused over what to tell them, her irate father, angry that she should have forsaken her cavernous world, appeared on the scene. He used his magical powers to put the giants into a deep trancelike sleep and ordered her back home. But Tamara was a feisty young lady, not one to be bossed about, and she refused, point blank, to accompany him. Her father's anger soared past breaking point and he cast a spell on her, which immediately turned her into a river, the mighty Tamar. Now in her new liquid form she flowed over the landscape, filling valleys as she twisted ever onward towards the sea, often bathed in the sparkling sunlight that she adored so much.

Tavy was the first of the two giants to wake and, after some basic detective work, found out what had happened to his beloved Tamara. He went home to his father, who was both a giant and a magician rolled into one mighty talent. He was also a sympathetic and compassionate character so reluctantly agreed to turn his son into the river Tavy that we know and love today. Speedily, and we can see this is a fast river, Tavy went in pursuit of his loved one, eventually to join her where their waters now intermingle at Bere Ferrers. Alas, poor Torridge fared less well, waking up too late and, having found a bungling magician, was dispatched the wrong way, turning away from Tamar to reach the sea on Devon's north coast.

A close look at a map soon reveals that this elevated tableland, where the Tavy rises, is the birthplace of many other streams and rivers; close to 'South Tavy Head' the Cowsic, Walkham, and West Dart also begin as infant trickles. People who know Tavistock reckon it rains far too much there, but the high rainfall figures for this rooftop of Dartmoor make Tavistock, farther down the Tavy valley, look positively dry in comparison!

There are few distinct landmarks, Fur Tor's granite mass, also known as the 'Queen of Dartmoor Tors', being the most obvious. For many years people have trekked to it on New Year's Day, trying to be the first of the year to sign the visitor's or 'letterbox' book. In 1995, to cite just one example, amongst the many 'letterboxers' who reached there were the 'Pink Panthers', 'The Travelling Bishops', 'The Hawk Boxers', 'Katie and Andy "on tor" on Dartmoor', 'The

Menheniot Maidens', 'Hissing Sid and Co' and 'Roomtrad' (I wonder if they walk backwards as well in order to live up to their name?). So, to be the first of the year to 'sign in' is indeed an achievement. This letterbox was established by the City of Plymouth Boy Scouts Association in October 1957, with the permission of the Duchy of Cornwall. However it took something of an initial battering from the elements and when Captain J. Joyner of the Junior Leaders Regiment, the Royal Signals (originators of the first 'Ten Tors Expedition' in 1960), found the box, a few years later, the stamp had gone missing and the book was in a sorry state. A group of officers, Norwegian apprentices and Junior Leaders revisited Fur Tor to replace the stamp and the book with more durable ones. They then posted the original book to the Plymouth Library, where completed books are housed to accompany those for Cranmere Pool, Crow Tor and Ducks Pool. Should you be a past 'peaty plodder' to the far horizons of Fur Tor then you can, should you wish, check your entry in the Local Studies section of this library, although some entries and pages have 'weathered' into oblivion.

The upper Tavy has various tributaries including the Fur Tor Brook and the Eastern Red Lake. In this context 'lake', a common term on the moor, means a stream. The river's first major confluence is at Sandy Ford where the Amicombe Brook adds its boisterous waters. This moorland watercourse has an extremely wet catchment area and is itself boosted by some 'lively' streams.

Although today this landscape is devoid of inhabitants, this hasn't always been the case, for a sizeable settlement, in late Bronze Age terms, once existed on the slopes of nearby Watern Oke. Some 80 or so 'houses' were discovered here when the site was fully excavated in 1905.

Not far from here yet another lively tributary stream adds its flow. The Rattle Brook, dancing down trout-laden from Amicombe Hill, rises on the heights of Woodcock Hill, its headwaters once the place of extensive peat working, to flow southwards to its confluence with the Tavy. The river, now given another boost, heads for canyon country, and on through the most spectacular section of its impressive valley. The Tavy, which drops a thousand feet in its first seven miles, is at its wildest in this, the most youthful moorland miles of its course. In a short distance it reaches one of the most striking parts of a stunningly beautiful county. Samuel Rowe, former vicar of Crediton, had this to say of it in his *Perambulation of Dartmoor*, first published in 1848: *"Still following the course of the Tavy downwards we shall soon reach the Tavy Cleave, a magnificent range of castellated tors with which nature appears to have fortified this fine peninsular hill, while the rapid stream sweeps around the headland, and forms an effective moat to the Titanic citadel above. There are five principal piles, of which the third is the loftiest and most majestic, and the whole cliff presents a remarkable resemblance to the dilapidated walls of a time-worn edifice."*

However, despite this magnificent scenery, living here was not a 'bed of roses', if William Crossing was correct. In his *Guide to Dartmoor* he referred to another ancient settlement, sited in a hollow opposite the Tavy Cleave Tors, where 'backalong', a term of intentional vagueness, those who lived here were driven out by the 'Evil One', who bellowed so loudly at night that they could not sleep. There is a weir, on the Tavy, which was referred to as 'Devil's Point', so perhaps these long-gone residents may have been wise to have vacated the area.

Had this been more recent times the noise may have been attributed to the military's presence, for the Tavy Cleave is within the Willsworthy Firing Range. If red flags are flying, from prominent hills, this valley is out of bounds to walkers. In 1900 the War Office purchased the manor of Willsworthy from the Calmady-Hamlyn family, allowing them to establish a 3,200 acre field-firing range. There is also a rifle range and the butts will be seen near White Hill.

The river's dramatic loss of height through the Tavy Cleave can largely be put down to the geology of the valley. The Tavy has cut down deep into its rocky bed because the horizontal and vertical joints in the granite are close together. In the valley bottom the solid granite forms oblong blocks and the river flowing along passes over a series of step-like waterfalls.

The Rev Sabine Baring-Gould had this to say of it in *A Book of Devon*, first published in 1899: *"Tavy Cleave is fine from below, but incomparably finer when seen from above.*

In June it is a veritable pixy fruit garden for luxuriance and abundance of purple whortleberries."

The Tavy's waters have been used by various mining enterprises. A good example is the multi-named Reddaford, Devon Friendship or more simply 'Mine' Leat. Many walkers reach the Tavy Cleave by following this leat around the hillsides, the easiest and best way to get there. A walk along this leat is also featured in *Ten Family Walks on Dartmoor*.

Many who have walked this way have commented on the optical illusion caused by the leat keeping its height whilst the land and the Tavy fall away. The leat thus appears to flow uphill but it can't really defy gravity and doesn't, so don't believe your eyes! And it's not so obvious an illusion as the Electric Brae, a hill near Ayr, in Scotland where cars can roll uphill, or so it seems.

If ever we needed a reminder that we were in the largest parish in England, this being Lydford, it is at the ford called Standon Steps. Those unfortunate enough to have died in the far-flung parts of this immense parish, covering much of the wilder parts of the moor, were carried over the Tavy at this point. The crossing was formed of wide stepping-stones strategically sited and perfectly placed to permit the body bearers to proceed in a dignified gait and two abreast, something not

Along The Tavy

easily possible on other Dartmoor stepping stones. However, during the Second World War, German prisoners of war were engaged in building a footbridge on top of the stones. This was

done to enable Jack Evans, of Standon, to cross the river even when it was in flood. As the range-clearer at Willsworthy, it was essential for him to be able to get across. After the war the bridge was damaged by floods but rebuilt by the MOD.

This location was the favoured crossing point for funeral parties after heavy rain. At other times processions crossed about a quarter of a mile downstream, where the Baggator Brook joins the Tavy, at another ancient crossing place. Here there are also stepping-stones, Cataloo Steps, and a ford,

both of which are of little use after prolonged heavy rain. The Tavy is one of those rivers that you have to treat with great respect.

The nearby Coffin Wood suggests that it has something to do with the Lich Way or 'The Way of the Dead', coming from *leich*, the German word for 'corpse' (there is also a Corpse Lane in the vicinity). There has been some debate as to whether coffins or, as some say, body sacks were used, but both notions may be wrong. The story, passed down through generations, is that it was the normal practice just to sling the body of the deceased unceremoniously over the back of a packhorse.

However, as time wore on it was felt that this was not showing sufficient respect to the dead or their families. It is suggested that Coffin Wood derived its name from the fact that a coffin was brought out to here, probably from Lydford. The corpse was then placed in it for the last leg of the journey to its final resting place at Lydford's parish church. Or could it be that the wood bears a similarity in shape to that of a coffin and the story is a myth?

Whichever route was taken it's likely that any funeral procession, long ago, would have stopped for a short while at a former small and somewhat basic chapel at Willsworthy, close to the Willsworthy Brook, a tributary of the Tavy. In a directory for 1850 it was described as "An ancient chapel which has long been used as a cowhouse".

Hill Bridge, built close to where there were originally stepping-stones, is the first road bridge to span the Tavy as it rushes on, dropping ever downwards, from its home-land in the Dartmoor alps In 1880 a spectacular storm produced a deluge in the upper reaches of the Tavy and both Hill Bridge and Mary Tavy Clam, further downstream, were washed away by the swift current.

The replacement bridge, the one we see today, was described by William Crossing as "... *a structure which, although not of so interesting a character as the one it replaces, is not wanting in the picturesque, whilst its surroundings cannot fail to delight. There is a happy mingling of trees, and fields, rock and river, of gorse and fern-clad banks, and above rise the hills of the moor*".

Cudlipptown, a terrific name, which sometimes seems to be spelt with one 'p' and other times two, is an ancient sub-manor, on the side of the Tavy valley, which belonged to Tavistock Abbey. It is one of those historical quirks that this hamlet remained part of the parish of Tavistock until the end of the nineteenth century despite being surrounded by the parishes of Peter Tavy and Mary Tavy.

The roads in this immediate district were never designed for motorists to get from A to B in a straight line, which is just as well as these quiet lanes are best suited to the indigenous population of the Tavy valley and, of course, those who visit to appreciate its charms. These lanes seem to delight in taking travellers on the most circuitous route imaginable.

Many folk head for the Elephant's Nest, formerly the New Inn, at Horndon, or 'Miners Town' as it was referred to in Victorian times. Names change, sometimes for good reasons. The hamlet of Horndon is now a peaceful one, the miners long gone, whilst the change of name to the 'Elephant's Nest' is one of those more imaginative ones. Originally it was three miners' cottages but these were converted into a large farm-house. About 1900 it became the New Inn (with Mr Reynolds as landlord), a name chosen because another, the now defunct Black Lion, was already well established. It is believed that it became the Elephant's Nest in 1952. Various versions of this story have been written or broadcast but the consensus seems to suggest that the pub once had an extremely large landlord who chose to perch on a stool and looked every bit like an elephant sitting on a nest, and so the change of name was effected.

The waters of the Tavy have been used for a great number of enterprises. In 1932 the West Devon Mining & Power Company, on the site of premises owned by Wheal Jewell and Mary Tavy Mines Ltd, established a hydroelectric power station, one of three schemes in Devon, the other two being at Morwellham and Chagford.

In 1980 a new two-storey building was erected without planning permission and, as you might have expected, was not greeted with universal approval. Consequently the top storey had to be removed. Two years later the HEP plant celebrated 50 years of service, a golden jubilee marked by the unveiling of a plaque in the presence of many past and present workers.

The plant, close to where the Cholwell Brook at Mary Tavy unites with the larger Tavy, is a small, efficient, and environmentally friendly one. There is a small reservoir on Kingsett Down, with an unusual shape which holds about 6,000,000 gallons of water. The construction of this obliterated the site of the former Wheal Jewell. An additional feeder leat is taken from the Tavy at Hill Bridge. Having produced the electricity all the waters gush back into the Cholwell Brook, boosting the flow for its last fling before merging with the nearby Tavy.

Between Hill Bridge and its confluence with the Cholwell Brook the Tavy heads very much in a south-westerly direction passing below Creason Wood and under Horndon Bridge. In its next miles many disused mines are passed, including North Devon United Mine, Central Devon United Mine and, true to form, South Devon United Mine. It also flows under some of the least-known of Dartmoor's tors, ones which you can read about in

Terry Bound's comprehensive *The A to Z of Dartmoor Tors*. For the record these piles, all above the north-western bank, on private land and often in vegetation, are Brimhill Tor, Kent's Tor, Fox Tor and High Tor. Longtimber Tor bucks the trend by being on the south-eastern bank, close to where the Tavy is joined by the Cholwell Brook. Anyone who walks the quiet road, which contours the valley side for most of the way, from Wapsworthy to Cudlipptown and beyond to Peter Tavy, will enjoy good views of this part of the valley.

Mary Tavy (an all-embracing name to include Blackdown and outlying farmsteads) is a sprawling settlement of about a thousand people, which is a lot less than in the mid-nineteenth century when there was plenty of work available in the district.

We have already mentioned some of the former mines but the principal one was Devon Friendship, an important copper mine just east of the village. It is virtually impossible to comprehend the network of subterranean workings that existed here, some at more than 200 fathoms or 1,200 feet. As with all mines, fortunes fluctuated and Devon Friendship saw both good times and bad. It started producing copper and lead in the early nineteenth century but closed, only to be reopened again later that same century, this time by the celebrated John Taylor in tandem with his sons. The firm developed and in the middle of the nineteenth century had expanded to employ a workforce of about 150. The once-lucrative copper mining became unprofitable in the 1870s and, although the mine struggled on, it became a non-viable venture and copper mining stopped. Nevertheless this operation had produced more than 160,000 tons of copper ore in its working life (plus 7,053 tons of pyrite, and notable amounts of lead, silver, zinc and scheelite). However, even after the demise of the copper ore mining there was still reduced employment, notably in the production of arsenic and tin ore, where activities continued, intermittently, into the twentieth century. But all now remains eerily silent, a long time having elapsed since miners stood at the bottom of a shaft to wait for pasties to be tossed down to them from great heights. The pasty was so designed, with the pastry not too short, that it could withstand the fall without disintegrating on or before impact.

Mary Tavy's church of St Mary is the last resting place of the famous Dartmoor writer William Crossing, whose works, so long after his death in 1928, still bring great joy to new generations of Dartmoor readers. He is buried with his wife in the north-east corner of the churchyard.

Like that of most other writers of local books, his work was a labour of love rather than one of any great financial gain. In his later life he fell on hard times but found a 'Guardian Angel' in the kind-hearted William Palmer Collins, who owned a cottage at Mary Tavy, in which he allowed Crossing to live rent-free. He even paid him to teach English and the Classics to two of his sons, Jack and Ronald. A small close in Mary Tavy is named after William Crossing, and there are other memorials to him, like the letter-box at Ducks Pool on Southern Dartmoor. This is covered in much greater detail in another of my books, *Cranmere Pool – The First Dartmoor Letterbox,* which really ought to be any letterboxer's first Dartmoor book!

There are some unusual graves and memorials here. Several combatants from the Civil War (1642–1646) were laid to rest beneath the Dartmoor hills. Their names were recorded with the word *miles* tagged on. This indicated that the dead man was a soldier. One entry, for 15 January 1643, lists *'Miles incognitus'*, an unknown soldier. In the time of the Commonwealth, following this conflict, one of the vicars to serve here was the Rev Thomas Jackson, a man who was driven to despair on being removed from his post. So troubled was he that he committed suicide and it is believed that he is still around, haunting the rectory and nearby area.

There is also a memorial to a man who died after wounds received whilst participating in a particularly brutal form of wrestling. John Hawkins played a game where opponents held on to each other's shoulders whilst trying to kick each other in the shins. Toughened toe-caps meant that participants often experienced crippling injuries, or worse.

The graveyard also contains several graves of people killed in mining accidents, some of them young. In the first half of the nineteenth century many children were employed at nearby Devon Friendship, several of whom didn't make 'old bones'.

Apparently, if you ask locals how far it is from Mary to Peter Tavy you will get conflicting answers. This is probably because some will travel between the two places on foot whilst others will do so by car. Even in the pre-motor age, Rachel Evans, writing in the 1840s, had this to say about the distance: *"The villages are only half a mile apart, so the miners say, but it may be a Cornish half mile, which is half as long again as a Devonshire one!"* By car, from the church of St Mary to that of St Peter it is about 2¹/₂ miles, almost five times as far, another example of acute indirectness.

There is a quiet and pleasant deep, steep-sided valley, bearing a small moorland stream, the Peter Tavy Brook, which runs into the Tavy on its east side at Peter Tavy. Within it are a number of farms, including Higher and Lower Godsworthy and, higher up the valley, towards its head, Wedlake. Although one could hardly find a more peaceful haven, this was the scene of a dispute, in February 1936, which led to a five-day protracted case at the Devon Assize in Exeter. The argument was over access for the plaintiffs, the Bellamys and Frederick J. Heywood of Wedlake.

To get to Wedlake the obvious way was along the track passing Lower Godsworthy, the home of the defendant Cyril George Abel. The case considered the moot point of access and both sides strove to show that a right of way existed, or didn't, something all too common these days with people stridently fighting either for their rights or for their privacy.

The case came to court primarily because Mr C. G. Abel had erected a gate across the lane denying access to Wedlake. When challenged Mr Abel had suggested that access to Wedlake lay via either of two paths, one known as Cox Tor, the other Twist Lane. However, the plaintiffs had an entirely different perspective on the matter.

Poor Mr Justice Hawke must have been bewildered at the procession of Peter Tavy personnel who came to have their 'fourpennyworth' in the public arena. The press reported the case in great detail and the judge, according to the headline in the regional paper, sat through it "As Though in a Dream".

The plaintiffs produced local folk who had had cause to visit the farm, or the open moor beyond, for work, for deliveries, for pleasure or for simply domestic reasons, never experiencing problems of access. Conversely the defendant's witnesses claimed that they had been challenged for having used this route. Celebrated Dartmoor writer Richard Hansford Worth, an expert on the use of local tracks and pathways, also gave evidence to the effect that he had used the road without problem on several occasions when carrying out a geological survey on the area of moor above Wedlake.

The judge found in favour of the plaintiffs, being satisfied that the occupants of Wedlake had had uninterrupted use of the road. He granted the declaration and injunction they had asked for and awarded them nominal damages of £4.7s.6d.

Judges are, of course, people of great wisdom but sometimes they can make fundamental mistakes. In another case, this time involving a land dispute which affected both Mary Tavy and Peter Tavy, the judge fell foul of local place names. Gazing down at the copious notes prepared for him he "confounded the names of the villages with those of the witnesses", and the usher was sent to call "Peter Tavy and Mary Tavy draw near and give your attendance".

Serious crime is rare in this area but in 1892 the peace and quiet of this part of the Tavy Valley was shattered. Young Eunice Doidge (known as 'Emma') was an attractive girl of just nineteen who turned many heads in the locality. There were plenty of young men who would have liked to walk out with her, and there were those 'lucky' ones who had. One of them, William Williams, had been cast off, his attentions no longer required as of June that fateful year. This had a profound effect on him and his behaviour was erratic to say the least. It was obvious, to most people in the Peter Tavy district, that the break-up of what he considered a romance would affect his health, as he had a past history of epilepsy. But nobody would have dared to imagine to what lengths he would go to in finding his own solution to his rejection.

Like many in similar communities, Emma was heavily involved in the life of the local church, being a member of the choir and a participant in bible classes; and, come rain or shine, she would always attend evening services at Peter Tavy's church, where her father was churchwarden.

Following such a service on Sunday, 13 November 1892, the congregation dispersed, many having quite a long walk along dark lanes to their outlying homes. Emma's long journey back to her home at Cox Tor Farm was one which would have seemed shorter in company. Emma stood outside the church talking to friends when Williams caused a commotion, spoiling for a fight, but was sent packing. However, none of the assembled group were aware that concealed on his person was a revolver which he had bought in Tavistock "To shoot a dog".

Williams stormed off into the night muttering threats and no doubt Emma and her escort, William Rowe, would have had plenty to discuss as they walked along the dark lanes climbing towards her home on the edge of the open moor. Tragically she was never to reach that sanctuary, for William Williams ambushed the couple, shooting both of them in the head before turning the gun on himself. Emma was killed instantly, William Rowe died the next morning, but Williams was merely stunned. He got to his feet and made his way to Harford Bridge, spanning the Tavy downstream from Peter Tavy. Here he tried to drown himself by plunging into the icy waters but, when he came around, found himself perched on a rock. In quite a state he hauled himself out of the river and banged on the door of Harford Bridge Cottage, explaining to the owner, in an almost incoherent fashion, what he had done. It was from here that the police later collected him.

The next day a bullet was removed from his neck at Tavistock's Cottage Hospital, and over the following days he began to make a recovery sufficient for him to be taken to Exeter, where he later stood trial for murder. He pleaded 'Not Guilty' and his defence tried to show that the killings were committed when he was not in a fit state of mind. His childhood epilepsy, and the mental ill health also in his family, were cited as reasons for determining a lenient sentence. Public feeling ran high and a petition, signed by more than 12,000 people, endorsed a similar sentiment that penal servitude would be an appropriate punishment. The judge, however, wasn't swayed by public opinion and sentenced Williams to death by hanging, this being carried out at Exeter. It brought the whole sorry saga to a conclusion with the death of a third young person from this quiet community, where unlawful acts are fortunately so few and far between. William Rowe's father was grief-stricken by the murder of his son. Although Joseph Rowe died from a heart and lung complaint, later that same year, there were those who suggested it was more from a broken heart.

Another example of domestic discord in Peter Tavy, on a much smaller scale, was evident in 1928 when Harewood House was built. Frank Bryant and his sister, who had married to become Mrs Fox, had grown up as the children of the rector of Peter Tavy, the Rev Francis John Bryant. Frank had married a 'sophisticated' London lady whilst his sister had married a local man. Frank and his sister, with the agreement of their respective partners, decided to build Harewood House and considerable thought went into its design. Frank was a passionate billiards player and his sister's husband, George Fox, was enthusiastic about playing the organ. Each insisted on having a room specially built for their favourite pastimes. The other rooms, which included seven bedrooms, were worked in around these whims.

George had an aversion to motor cars and was worried that if they came too close to the house they might shake his cameras, so the double garage was built about a minute's walk from the premises.

However, Frank Bryant had a few problems: his wife refused to live in or even visit Dartmoor, no doubt thinking of it as a social backwater; and he found it difficult to get on with his brother-in-law. For these reasons Frank never spent any significant time in his part of the house, which sounds as if it might have been the more comfortable section, since it had central heating and George's half didn't!

So whilst Mr and Mrs Fox lived their austere existence, Mr and Mrs Bryant opted to reside in London. In 1939 George died so in 1940 Frank, who had spent a great deal of time abroad in warmer climes, made a rare visit to Peter Tavy. He was not at all happy to discover that his sister had rented out the property at £1 per week. It was to be another nineteen years before his family got full possession but this was no consolation to Frank as he had passed on! However, his granddaughter, Mrs Guest, moved in to live there and many Peter Tavy folk will, no doubt, have fond memories of attending concerts, plays or charitable events held at Harewood House in those postwar years.

The village church contains a sad epitaph to the early seventeenth century family of former rector, Reverend Eveleigh. His five daughters all died in infancy, none of them more than a year old. They are remembered with these words: "They breath'd awhile and look't ye world about, And like new-lighted candles soone went out."

Peter Tavy's church was not the place to be on 2 November 1803, particularly if you were brontophobic, tonitrophobic or astrophobic, because Dartmoor, often referred to as 'The Land of Thunder', lived up to its name. A ferocious storm reverberated around the granite hills, striking terror into the hearts of those with a nervous disposition. The storm homed in on this moorland-edge village and, as is so often the case, a thunderbolt sought out the highest point of the pinnacles of the church, causing much damage. Happily, unlike at Widecombe on 21 October 1638, where the storm was blamed on the Devil, nobody was killed or maimed by the blast.

It was more a case of the 'Demon Drink' rather than the Devil that concerned a Peter Tavy vicar of yesteryear. William Crossing first told this story in 1901, featuring an example of the ultimate 'treading on eggshells'. Imagine the dilemma facing churchwarden Roger Mudge, a man of conscience who did not wish to upset anyone.

The Rev Mr McBean suspected that his congregation was being reduced by those who preferred to be in the pub whilst the morning service was being conducted. So he dispatched Roger to check out the situation. This was a task that he wouldn't enjoy, for he had no wish to upset the landlord of the Peter Tavy Inn, as he was one of his own relations, but, at the same time, he could not lie to the vicar. A compromise was arranged so as he would not have to lie. He would approach the pub so slowly and deliberately that everyone knew that he was coming. Roger fixed his gaze

straight ahead, and did not dare to look into the pub's windows for fear of seeing anyone inside. To make completely sure, he would repeatedly utter, getting louder with each encroaching step, "I'm coming, cousin Tom". Whilst this weekly ritual was going on, those who had been 'guilty' of drinking or church dodging secreted themselves away in a back room. Roger would tentatively enter, gaze around and, seeing nobody there, be happy to report back to the parson that the inn was devoid of potential churchgoers, his honour and integrity intact, at least technically.

The reputation of Peter Tavy men and their drinking sessions was recorded on paper thus by the Victorian writer Rachel Evans: *"Some years since I remember going to the church at Peter Tavy on a Revel Sunday. My feelings are best expressed by saying that, although but a child I was ashamed to be there. Standings for fairings and toys were erected in close vicinity to the churchyard; parties were engaged in noisy vociferations over their favourite game of kayles (or nine pins); shouts of drunken laughter came from the village inn, and even at an early hour men passed along in a state of intoxication."*

Rumour has it that one of HMP Dartmoor's most notorious former prisoners, Frank Mitchell, alias 'The Mad Axeman', was a frequent visitor to this inn, and this when he was supposed to be 'banged up'. The rumour was extended to suggest that his bar tab was picked up by one of the Kray twins, the cheque to cover it being pinned to one of the timbered ceiling beams in this fifteenth century inn. For the record, it's possible that this burly, dangerous man could have visited the pub, for he was a member of an 'honour party' being allowed to work outside with a degree of freedom, but just how much has been the subject of many discussions and enquiries. We know that his bid

for even greater freedom began when he walked away from a hut on Bagga Tor, in the Tavy valley, on 12 December 1966. He 'announced' that he was going to feed ponies about half a mile away but was never seen again! His clothes were found about 30 miles away at Crockernwell, a small village that used to be on the A30 before the current route bypassed it. After this even more rumours prevailed about his 'lavish' lifestyle. The consensus of opinion seems to suggest that he was helped to escape and then murdered and, if the urban folk tale is to be believed, he is set in concrete in a motorway bridge...

Near Harford Bridge, one of two within the Dartmoor National Park (the other Harford Bridge spans the Erme a few miles above Ivybridge), is a complex of buildings that was once a sugar factory. Since its less than sweet passing a number of speculative ventures have foundered there for a variety of reasons. In December 1992 it was hoped to stage a youth performed pantomime, a festive version of *Hansel and Gretel*. However, the Devon and Cornwall Police, amongst others, objected on various grounds to this being the venue. The five scheduled performances,

with an estimated audience of 500 at each house, never materialised, this proving to be a bitter pill to swallow for those keen to do it. Not too long afterwards the premises were planned to become an ambulance museum.

Beside Harford Bridge is an excellent caravan park, the perfect spot for those who want to explore the Tavy and surrounding district.

The Tavy now flows below the immense Pitts Cleave Quarry and heads past the Trout 'N' Tipple pub, formerly the Cottage Inn, and on towards Tavistock, but first it passes between two schools, one on each side of the valley, both wise enough to be built on elevated ground.

During the First World War 'Mount Tavy', on the east bank, became the Tavistock Neurological Hospital, opening its door to many hundreds of shell-shocked victims of the battlefields of Belgium and France. Those fit enough were placed on the farms in the district, in the hope that the relatively peaceful pursuits of the country would rehabilitate them following their harrowing experiences in trench warfare. These troops were often seen in the town wearing a light-blue uniform.

Tavistock has seen its share of famous people and Kelly College, opened on 25 October 1876, has certainly educated some household names. Sharron Davies, swimming star, former Gladiator and television presenter, is just one well-known person who went to school here.

The college, designed by Charles Hanson and John Pethick, derives its name from Admiral Benedictus Marwood Kelly, native of Holsworthy, who posthumously funded, on a site given by the Duke of Bedford, a school "for the sons of naval officers and other gentlemen".

It has had some colourful headmasters. Some may remember Commander Rupert Vyvyan Hawksley, who had been head at West Buckland School from 1934 to 1938. But rather than 'To Serve Them All My Days' (R. F. Delderfield was at the same school in the same era!) he came to Kelly College in 1939, and was headmaster for some twenty years. He ran the place almost single-handed and established his own tradition of insisting that any boy's mother, who came to visit a son, had to kiss the headmaster before leaving the site.

The first bridge reached in Tavistock is a modern structure called Stannary Bridge, a reflection of the role the town played in the tin industry (the word *stannum* is Latin for tin). It's not a thing of beauty but it performs its intended function. A passing motorist new to the area would not notice the Tavy flowing below, which was a major part of the town's original reason for being here. A short way downstream is the unusually named Vigo Bridge, the narrowest one to span the river in the town.

Tavistock, the famous and ancient Stannary Town, was sited close to the Tavy to enjoy its advantages and to tolerate its watery whims for, as we have seen and are yet to see, it can be a mean and merciless neighbour. Bridging the river has always been a challenge and over the years there have

been various bridges spanning it. Changes to the townscape and layout, and changes in traffic, have seen different bridges come and go. The narrow, medieval five-arched 'Great Bridge' (also referred to as Guild or, later, East Bridge) is no longer with us, having stood, for half a millennium, at a point between the Abbey and Vigo Bridges. It was replaced in 1764 by the aptly-named, humpback Abbey Bridge, part of the improved road network of the turnpikes. However, this structure was adapted to changing needs and was also widened and improved after the arrival of the railway to the town.

There are some unusual names in Tavistock, just one of them being Dolvin Road, a thoroughfare running beside the Tavy. One possible interpretation is that the name is a shortened corruption of Godolphin, the name of an eminent family in the area.

Buried in the Dolvin Road Cemetery are some whose lives were lost in the building of the now disused railroad which ran above this gothic graveyard.

It rains a lot in Tavistock, or so the locals claim, but even King Charles I was known to joke about it. If someone commented on it being a fine day he would automatically reply, "But it is undoubtedly raining at Tavistock!" Sometimes the heavens just open up to produce so much precipitation that a flash flood is created. There have been several such inundations, the Tavy rising many feet in a short time. Indeed, it is reckoned that the Tavy is the second quickest river in England in its rise after prolonged rain.

Some of the Tavy's lesser tributary streams have also had their moments. The diminutive Tiddybrook, which rises on Whitchurch Down, caused some problems in late May 1981 when it rose from its normal depth of about six inches to an incredible eight feet in just half an hour and washed a car away, appropriately a Ford, and flooded many buildings including Anderton Court.

The Tavy has caused numerous floods over the years. Beneath Tavistock's police station, in low-lying Bedford Square, there were seven dungeon-like cells. On 17 July 1890, during a terrific thunderstorm, one prisoner held there got very worried, as the Tavy had burst its banks and his cell started filling up with flood water. Luckily his worst nightmare was ended when the police came down to extricate him just 'in the nick' of time! That thunderstorm wreaked havoc on the western side of the moor, the rivers Cowsic and Walkham showing similar sharp rises in level of many feet. Double Waters, downstream, where the Tavy is joined by the Walkham, must have been an amazing sight at eight o'clock that morning when the 'tide' was at its height. However, as is often the way, the river levels dropped almost as fast as they had risen. Nevertheless there was considerable damage caused by the flood: the Mary Tavy Clam was washed away for a second time in 'recent years'; Harford Bridge lost one of its arches; and in Tavistock the canal weir was washed away – the river, having both volume and speed, was a merciless force sweeping everything before it.

Ten years before, another inundation was destined to cause a major disaster, which we will feature later, the floods again turning Bedford Square into a miniature version of Venice. The town stocks, so much a part of practical justice in the past, had been tethered to a rope. The current lifted this heavy wooden apparatus and had they not been secured they would have sailed away. Fortunately nobody was in them at the time.

The Tavy is said to influence the very nature of the local population. J. Henry Harris in his *My Devonshire Book* (1907), full of quirky comments, wrote this: *"Everything considered, the town of Tavistock has been of very slow growth. A first-class liner would take the whole population to America, and yet the town seems always to have been prosperous, and to have given birth to men of energy and ambition. A stranger leaning against the parapet of the ancient ivy-covered bridge sees only a little more, of the 'gossips' of other days. The bridge is the great attraction, and some people say that the tumultuous, whirling, brawling river as it passes has played its share in moulding the character of the people who aforetime passed their time in hanging over it, and listening to its music."*

Arthur H. Norway in his *Highways and Byways in Devon and Cornwall* also cited the bridge as being responsible for other human traits, when this appeared in an early edition of his often republished work: *"The bridge is the true centre of the town of Tavistock, a wondrous place for reflection and romance. It was long since pointed out by qualified observers that a bridge across a running stream conduces to idleness. Yes, but much comes of idleness in such a spot as this. Here idleness is a virtue; and he is a bad man who hastens by with no more than a passing thought for the brown water foaming under the old bridge, the dark pools round which it swirls, the trailing ivy which hangs in the cool shadow of the arches, the weir over which the river boils a few yards further on, the salmon ladder by its side, and the leaping of the fish in the still pool beyond, where the rush and turmoil of the fall is carried under water by its own weight and the foam and bubbles may be seen glistening below the unrippled surface. Black and broken by white rapids, the river hastens on, flashing over boulders beneath an avenue of high elm trees, through which the hot sunshine dapples on the water; and so sweeping sidewards is lost among the meadows where, until the floods of two winters since, there stood a hollow oak tree known as 'Lady Howard's Oak'. For here, too, the stories of that grim old woman intrude themselves; and it only needs an effort to cast them all aside a while, and follow the course of the old abbey walls, which from this side only retain their ancient aspect."*

William Crossing, who lived for years at Mary Tavy, knew the Tavy well, having walked 'almost every inch' of this Dartmoor river in his quest for knowledge. This is what he wrote in 1903: *"Leaving the town by the Abbey Walk, we shall make our way through the Meadows by the riverside path to the West Bridge. With the disappearance of Lady Howard's Oak, an ancient tree, which a storm unkindly brought down a few years ago, the path has lost perhaps a little of its interest; but fortunately nature has done so much for it that it needs no historic associations to render it attractive."*

It is likely that Crossing appreciated the open space of these meadows, for Tavistockians had used it as a meeting place for as long as most could remember. However, it was not always a public open space, the Urban District Council having had to go to great lengths to get a 21-year lease on it from the Duke of Bedford, from 1898. Even dukes sometimes have to 'rationalise' their financial affairs and the Bedfords' (family name Russell) ducal fortunes fell on relatively hard

times in 1911. The local corporation were able to acquire the lands in 1912. The correct name for this patch of recreational land, between the Tavistock Canal and the Tavy, was Jessop's Hay Meadow but, as this is a bit of mouthful, it has short-formed to The Meadows, an apt name.

Tavistock's second bridge, at the south-western end of this park, was the three-arched West Bridge, one which was replaced in 1939 by a wider single span close to the same spot as the original. The scene here, years ago, would have had a more industrial feel to it, for close to the forerunner of this bridge was the Crelake copper mine, whose workings dominated the landscape for many years.

The River Tavy passes the town's community college and continues on close to the home of Tavistock FC's Langsford Park ground. The only game I have seen this South Western League club play was on 10 August 1974 when my own hometown team, Exeter City, played there in a pre-season friendly, to celebrate the opening of new changing rooms, a match which the league club won. The most memorable incident, from a completely forgettable game, involved City player Lammie Robertson, who took a penalty. Unfortunately he spooned his attempt way above the crossbar, the ball ballooning high into the air before landing on the head of one of a number of unsuspecting Friesian cows (all sporting the colours of Newcastle United), which had been standing quietly watching the game. Fortunately for Exeter City, the same player netted four penalties in league games that season, human spectators being spared the same indignity.

Crowndale Meadows lie just below Tavistock, a series of large flat fields on the west bank of the River Tavy. In the past, before the annual Devon County Show settled on a fixed venue in or near Exeter, this location was occasionally used for Devon's prestigious agricultural event. Perhaps the decision to find a permanent venue was made after what happened in May 1932.

There was little portent of what was to come when the second day of the show dawned to bright, breezy sunny late spring-like conditions. The people of Devon looked out of their windows at pleasant conditions and dressed accordingly for a fine day at the show. If there was an odd shower or two it wouldn't matter. In that frame of mind many folks left their homes and farms to make their way across the county to the banks of the Tavy. However, it wasn't long before great black clouds rolled in off the Atlantic and a downpour of Dartmoor dimensions doused the show in the heaviest rain imaginable, and continued to do so all day.

The flat showfield could not absorb the water and those areas which were not churned up into mud, many inches deep, formed large pools of water.

The President of the show was Prince George, who had enjoyed a fine, sunny previous day in Cornwall. He spent the night as the guest of Sir Henry Lopes at Maristow, also on the banks of the Tavy but much farther downstream.

The Prince first paid an early morning visit to Kelly College before making the scheduled visit to the County Show, turning up more than half an hour early. He, too, had interpreted the weather wrongly and only wore dry weather gear. However, on entering the first tent he summoned more appropriate apparel and emerged with gum boots, mackintosh and umbrella. These enabled him to brave the elements for one and a half hours, his radiant smile being the one bright spot on the darkest of days, or so the press wrote in their editorial of the event. Prince George's first task was to inspect the local police force, the Devon County Constabulary, under the command of the Chief Constable, Major L. H. Morris. Some 200 police officers, from across the county, had been invited but the weather had turned so bad that many missed the inspection, one which finished with all the policemen taking off their helmets to give three enthusiastic cheers for His Royal Highness. After hearing of the absentees, the Prince kindly did another inspection of the police closer to lunch time.

By the end of the morning the ground conditions, for the crowd of some 5,795, were almost impassable, this being the quote from the next day's paper: *"The whole show-yard became a veritable bog, and the plight of people and animals was distressing in the extreme... Hundreds of womenfolk in light silk stockings splashed and floundered in the mud and the light mackintoshes could simply not withstand the deluge."* But what is it they say about every cloud? One stall, specialising in weatherproof items of clothing, did a roaring trade, so good in fact that by midday every single item that they had brought to the show had been sold.

There were lighter moments to punctuate the gloom. Prince George stopped to see a veteran hen, who duly obliged by laying her 1,025th egg, the first having been squeezed out some six years earlier in 1926. (I wonder who had been so 'eggsact' in counting?)

For the organisers, the show must have been a disaster for an earlier county show, staged in 1921 on the same site, had produced a crowd of 16,110. For them it had been the second year running that the second day had been almost a washout, for the previous year the Devon County Show staged at Tiverton had suffered a similar fate, but at Crowndale the morass transformed the event into a farce. The show is now staged at the fixed venue of Westpoint, Clyst St Mary in East Devon, the annual average rainfall being some 50 per cent less than that of Tavistock!

The watery theme continues with a disaster on 13 July 1880, at the now disused East Wheal Crebor Mine on the other bank of the Tavy opposite Crowndale Meadows.

Three Tavistock men, Henry Hill, William John Cloak and Thomas Allen, in a workforce of six, had gone off to work at this mine, which had recently reopened after years of dereliction. The men entered the mine at 2.00 p.m. to begin their shift, having seen for themselves a spectacular downpour of rain, even by Tavistock standards, late that morning. The Tavy had risen many feet, as was its custom, but the miners were not over-worried for they were about to enter their own dark labyrinthian world, usually divorced from that above ground. They probably assumed that by the time they finished their shift the storm would have passed and the level of the Tavy would have fallen again. And to some degree such logic was correct. However, somehow the Tavy, at its peak at about 4.00 p.m., penetrated the lower levels of this mine. Hill, Allen and Cloak had been working a level some 70 fathoms (420 feet) below the surface, whilst the other three miners were ten fathoms above them. The difference proved critical for the mine was to flood up to the 62 fathom level. By the time the miners had realised the peril of their situation it was too late. The three men mentioned by name were drowned, their bodies recovered the following day.

Beyond Shillamill Viaduct the road runs beside the Tavy for a short way before leaving the valley bottom behind to essay the steep and quaintly named Lazy Bench Hill. Above the road the map names 'Stoneage Rocks' but they are much older than that. The Tavy now becomes something of an antisocial river choosing to flow, out of the gaze of most folks, through a steep-sided, heavily wooded valley.

So far we haven't considered the river's residents, the fishes themselves. The aquatic life of the river is sometimes at the mercy of human kind who, by their actions, can have a major effect on fish stocks or the state of water quality in our rivers. An article on the subject was written by T. Agnew May for Crossing's *'The Western Gate of Dartmoor' – Tavistock and its Surroundings,* which was published in 1903. Here brief snippets of it have been included because they give an insight into the river's past setting, particularly the stretch below Tavistock. *"The parts of the Tavy open to the public... are the whole of the right bank from the weir next above Denham Bridge to its source; on the left bank, that portion between Wheal Bertha Mine and the Walkham; the portion between Tavistock Cemetery and Vigo Bridge, in Tavistock; from*

Harford Bridge to Mary Tavy Clam; from Horndon Clam to its source with the exception of a few fields... The Tavy is a marvellously prolific river for trout, and, though many small fish will be taken, many run to a respectable size, particularly below Tavistock, and fish of a pound and upwards are not unknown. Connoisseurs pronounce Tavy trout to be of a singularly delicious flavour... But the charms of the Tavy are not confined to its trout; it is an excellent peel (or sea trout) river and the kingly salmon is occasionally taken. By the way, how is it that nearly all the salmon that run up the joint estuary seem to select the Tamar, and nearly all the peel, the Tavy, as their breeding ground?

On the Tavy every considerable pool has its own particular name, and it will be sometimes found to be very useful to know some at least of these names... Some pools seem never without fish; the big deep pool at the old Virtuous Lady Mine is the most famous in the river, and probably more fish are pulled out of this pool than out of any of any other six put together.

It is a pity that the bushes are not cut systematically; much of the water is quite unfishable owing to the mass of growth overhanging it. This is especially the case from the Walkham junction up to the long pool known as Washford, just below the new Rifle Butts. Some of the best ground in the river has thus to be left untouched – wading being strictly prohibited – and nothing is more annoying than to see good fish on the move and to be absolutely unable to put a fly over them. Further it often happens that you get fast in a heavy peel in one of the few openings and then lose him through sheer inability to follow him in consequence in the dense undergrowth. Surely representations to the tenant farmers might produce good results...

The bugbear of fishermen in the Tavy is the mine. Some years ago all the fish, trout as well as migratory fish, from Wheal Bertha to the mouth, were killed by a so-called accident at this mine. Just now (1903) when the river has recovered from the effects of the last slaughter, fishermen are viewing with the greatest apprehension the proceedings of a new mine at Peter Tavy. Almost daily the water is much discoloured by the discharge from this mine, and the spawning beds are being gradually choked with the deposit. We have to our relief heard that catch-pits, or filter-beds are being made to intercept the solid matter, and can only express a hope that they may prove effectual; this can only be the case if they are kept thoroughly and systematically emptied of the deposit.

The lower parts of the Walkham are, like much of the Tavy, ruined from the fisherman's point of view by bushes, but at the same time a few openings can be discovered. This river will be found in excellent ply at times when the bigger stream is too heavy. Below Horrabridge it can be reached from that station."

Double Waters is the famed beauty spot, accessible on foot, where the Walkham pours its load into the Tavy. Close to this confluence are the disused workings of the Virtuous Lady Mine (474698). It is reputed that this mine was named in honour of Elizabeth I and the 1558 date of opening makes this a distinct possibility. The mine employed between 100 and 200 workers, depending on demand, before it closed down in 1807. However, in the 1830s it enjoyed a rebirth which was to see it enter its most productive time, with large amounts of copper ore mined in the middle of that century. At that time Rachel Evans wrote this of it: *"And surely no virtuous lady had ever a brighter hue than this. There are*

crystal gems around her on every side; a small rill forms a sparkling cascade as it bounds from the hill tops to turn the works of the mine, and the waters of the Tavy below throw up pearly drops of every hue as they foam over the dam formed in ages long past and from some old association called the 'Abbot's Weir'; it is probable that the monks, catering for good cheer, constructed the dam for the convenience of fishing, in the time of the sainted abbot, who bestowed his benediction and name on the scene of their labours." She went on to add a description of the inside of this wondrous mine, which went down some 120 fathoms (720 feet). *"Within are preserved, safe from all injury, crystals, rising like some precious plant with tubercles of copper for their root. Nor are these the only treasures of this most eccentric mine. Capped spar or quartz; and the most beautiful specimens of copper are here raised. No one will regret a visit to this favoured nook, however difficult of access it may be. Strangers can enter the mine by an incline plane without much*

inconvenience. Many adventurous damsels have sought its hidden recesses and have traversed its gloomy passages lighted by a flickering candle to view the workmen in their gloomy gear boring like a mole through the deep caves of the earth...

Never having performed this feat myself, I can boast only of having ventured to the entrance of the mine to examine the original excavations made in ages long past... A cottage belonging to the captain of the mine is built on upon the edge of the cliff overlooking the Abbot's Weir, and commanding a beautiful prospect of the vale." Alas, she added a footnote saying: *"Since writing the above, the late, kind and obliging occupant of this cottage, Mr Martin, nephew of Captain Williams, and superintendent of the mine, has met with an awful and sudden death by the falling in of a shaft, which he was in the act of inspecting."* If experts can be killed in mines, then visiting amateurs would have had no chance, so don't even think of exploring old mines! Parts of the rest of her writings are worth quoting.

"A complete picture of the workings of the mine above ground, is seen by looking from the eminence on the platform by the river beneath. There are the pits in which the ore is washed; the various sheds in which it is sorted; and the stamping mills in which it is ground to powder; then the creaking of the machinery is heard as it bends to and fro. The water wheels too, are in constant motion. Men, women and children are actively employed. All around are profusely scattered some of the most romantic beauties of nature... The woods and rocks on the right bank of the river are singularly beautiful; they are gained by one of those picturesque clams or long wooden bridges formed of one plank ... so frequently thrown across our noisy streams..."

However, the fortunes of mining are fickle and Virtuous or not, this mine was no different to most others in the district and ceased working again in 1870, more than 40 people losing their livelihood on its closure.

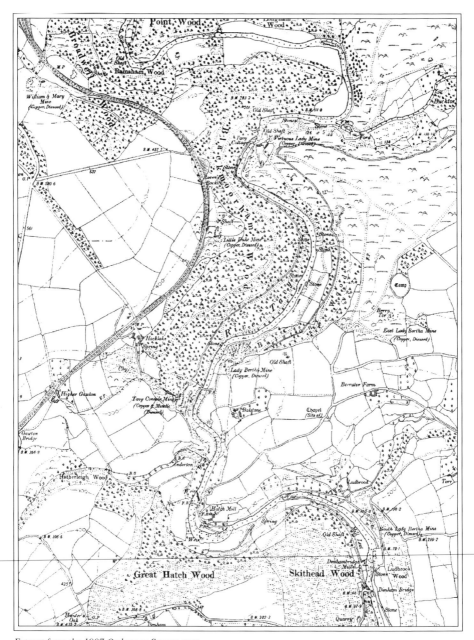

Extract from the 1907 Ordnance Survey map

Beyond Double Waters the river continues through much more of the same country of steep wooded hillsides, still shy of the public, as it passes more disused copper mines. The remains of Little Duke's mine are hidden away high on the shoulder of the hill in Blackmoorham Wood whilst further downstream, beside the Tavy, Lady Bertha stands neglected on the east bank. Tavy Consols is another long-defunct enterprise which also looks somewhat forlorn on the slope above the west bank. This mine was unusual in that tin and arsenic ores were found above copper ores, an apparent contradiction of the mineral zoning, which would be well-known to masters of metalliferous mineralisation but not to us lesser mortals. Looking at this lovely part of the now silent valley it's hard to imagine the great amount of activity which once took place here.

No previous mention has been made of the number of mills along the Tavy and, bearing in mind its strong and reliable flow, there have been many, particularly in the vicinity of Tavistock, to use its waters to good purpose. The remote, but beautifully sheltered, Hatch Mill is just one in this part of the valley. It had a reputation in the nineteenth century for turning out the best flour in the area. It ceased working in about 1906 but in its last years it only ground corn for cattle.

Hatch Ford was the scene of a disaster in 1791 when William Good and his young daughter, Elizabeth, sharing the same horse, attempted to cross the Tavy. The horse slipped and fell in the river. The father lost his life in trying to save his daughter. Both were classified as paupers in the burial records at nearby Buckland Monachorum's church.

The river runs around another great winding bend, over a series of weirs and beneath precipitous slopes to reach another mill, the former Denhambridge Mill. As I am a non-swimmer, an anti-paddling sign, near the granite packhorse Denham Bridge, which states that the river has pools 40 feet deep, strikes terror into my heart. The men who worked at the nearby South Lady Bertha copper mine, which closed in 1854, may well have washed away the grime and dust here after a shift, indeed an invigorating daily constitutional!

Beyond this beauty spot, where the narrow road climbs steeply up towards Bere Alston, the Tavy continues to twist in its deep, steep anciently-wooded valley as it heads on towards its estuary. The building of the dam at Lopwell resulted in foreshortening the estuary. The tidal limit once extended about another mile upstream of Lopwell to a point close to where a small stream, running down from Buckland Abbey, joins the Tavy. Apparently, there was once a small quay here, until the early twentieth century, where 'Dock dung' was 'imported' for use on the land. There was also an 'oasis' of agricultural land on the side of the Tavy valley known as the Terrace Meadows. About the only form of transport which could reach these shallows was the flat-bottomed Tamar barges. On return journeys downstream they took woodland-related products – firewood, bark, timber, beanpoles and so on.

Lopwell Dam was constructed in the mid-1950s to help augment Plymouth's water supply, and the water is pumped from here to the treatment works at Crownhill. If, on your first visit to this beauty spot, you have that feeling of *déjà-vu* then it might be explained if you are something of a tele-addict as, in the early 1990s, two series of *The Vet* were filmed around here. The Vet's surgery was here at Lopwell (originally Lophill), housed in the unlikely setting of the pumping house close to the weir. The building's 'fairly remote' location and the bonus of the beautiful

backcloth of Whittacliffe and Blindwell Woods made the film maker's job easier. The female vet's home was Riverside Cottages, beside the Tamar at Bere Ferrers, and these were holiday lets at that time. Other locations included Plymouth, Wembury, Cholwell, Tavistock and the lovely Milton Combe, just up the lane from Lopwell. The somewhat 'doom and gloom' first series was followed by a more cheery, light-hearted second series.

Along The Tavy

Lopwell was the location of a once-important quay where lead and silver were exported. Also here were the inevitable kilns, burning lime brought up from the Plymouth district to be used to sweeten the soil. Farmers queued at an unearthly hour to collect lime so hot that at times wooden carts would catch ablaze and be destroyed. There was also a working mill here until 1872. It is now a place where people come to enjoy a walk and, when the state of the tide permits, it's possible to cross the river to the Bere Ferrers side but those who linger too long have a long detour to get back to Lopwell Quay!

There is a narrow road which runs through parkland from Lopwell to nearby Maristow

where 'Chuck's Ford' is located. However, there was no guarantee of a safe crossing, as Rachel Evans wrote in 1846: *"A short time since a young surgeon was lost, in attempting to ford the stream in a gig, on a dark evening."* Fortunately the formation of extensive mud banks has rendered the 'ford' impassable now. The former tidal road, which ran along the foreshore, on the west bank of the Tavy, from Chucks Ford, past the former quay at Gnatham, to Bere Ferrers, was once the most direct trade route for wagons or carts carrying goods bound for the Plymouth markets.

There are so many places along the Tavy where it's hard to imagine any past industrial activity. Even here, in this idyllic spot, there was trade in the past. Silver, produced from the once-famous mines at Bere Ferrers, was also brought here before being taken on to the Treasury in London.

This hamlet was originally 'Martin's-stow' and, as the latter part of the name means 'church', it's not surprising to see that here we have the domestic St Martin's Chapel, the second on the site. When the first was demolished parts of its fabric were salvaged for the building of a folly in the grounds.

A number of famous families feature in the Maristow estate's history, including the Champernownes who were granted it after the Dissolution. It then passed on to the Slannings and then the Heywoods, who entertained the Royal Family here in the 1780s whilst they were staying at Saltram. King George III, Queen Charlotte and three Princesses made two visits. On the death of James Modyford Heywood the estates were bought in 1798 by the Jamaican-born Mannasseh Masseh Lopes. His father, Mordecai Rodriguez Lopes, had made a fortune as a sugar plantation owner before, having moved to the less exotic Clapham, setting down his roots in this country. His son, one-time MP for Romney, inherited his incredible fortune and this allowed him to acquire the manors of Bickleigh, Buckland Monachorum, Shaugh Prior, Maristow and Walkhampton, some 32,000 acres. This is most of the land featured in *Around & About Roborough Down*, one of the two companion books to this one, where there are, not surprisingly, further mentions of the Lopes family, whose members seemed to favour the letter 'M' in their Christian names,

at least in Victorian times. With their wealth, titles and influence, the Lopes family made a big impact on this area.

Their choice of home couldn't have been much better and the river was to play its part in the running of their estate. Up to the First World War, barges brought the goods and materials that the family required. However, the house has been the victim of some disastrous fires.

In more recent decades the house has seen a range of uses and users. During the Second World War it turned into a hospital, and since then it has been a field study centre and a residential home for the subnormal. For a while it became 'Heaven's Waiting Room', as it was a home for aged clergy. In 1997 this prestigious property, lovingly and expertly restored, became twelve luxury houses.

One of the best books about the area that I have ever read is *Under Sail Through South Devon and Dartmoor* by Raymond B. Cattell. This terrific book, first published in 1937, is a log of journeys done in a small two-seater canoe around the coast and up most of the rivers of South Devon. In it Ray visits the Dart, Avon, Erme, Yealm and finishes his voyage with the Tamar. However, he has this to say of the Tavy, as he saw it in the 1930s:

"Today we would explore the Tavy up to Tavistock. True the tide was all wrong, but we had been slaves of the tide long enough. Our unusually vigorous paddling unfortunately proved too much for Sandpiper. *She wept with a bad leak very soon and we had to find our way through gleaming mud banks, by a row of crazy posts in the river, to Bere Ferrers, a quiet, grey little river village, so beautifully situated that it might have been created as part and parcel of the woods and river themselves.*

The son of the house at the post office gave us his last patch with which to repair Sandpiper – *no mean sacrifice in so outlandish a place – but our warm feelings for Bere Ferrers were somewhat shaken by the imprecations and incantations of an old witch at the staithe. When I said 'I beg your pardon', she fixed me with the Evil Eye and announced that Tavy stream had drowned one soul every year, adding mincingly that this year she was rather late. She then settled down to watch our departure with an air of agreeable expectancy which fairly gave us what I believe is technically known as 'a fit of the Willy's'.*

The stream was very swift and as we approached Lopwell it brought us to a standstill, in spite of furious paddling. Something was wrong with our calculations, for the tide should now have been at the calm of the ebb. I have described how, in the Exe, the tide turns some hours later far up the river than at the mouth; but this was more than lateness.

At first I ascribed everything to the witch at Bere Ferrers, but on reading the newspaper next day I decided the uncanny circumstances were due to a cloudburst which had sent wheelbarrows floating down Tavistock streets that morning. At any rate we were beaten and had to cling to overhanging branches to save ourselves from being swept away. Some day I will tackle Tavy stream on the fullness of a spring tide into Tavistock itself; for natives of great judgment tell me that these deep, meandering and wooded gorges constitute the grandest scenery south of the moors."

But the eminent Professor Raymond B. Cattell is not the only one to have enjoyed 'fun and frolicking' on the Tavy, for the villagers of Bere Ferrers have held water sports festivals in, on and beside the river. Should you ever be in the vicinity at the right time you may see weird craft like the 'Loch Tavy Monster' parading in wondrous fashion. Tugs-of-war, crab fishing, slippery poles, boat races, welly-wanging, boat trips and many other river events have brought fun and a sense of community to this lovely 'peninsular' village.

According to *Kelly's Directory* of 1889 the church of St Andrew was the scene of a tragedy. This is what part of the entry said: *"... the east window is enriched with ancient stained glass, replaced in 1871, and comprising kneeling figures of Sir William Ferrers and Isota his wife; the knight holds a church in his hands, and over his head is the inscription 'WILLS FEREYS ME FECIT'; below are the shields of Ferrers and Carminow: on May 28th, 1821, Charles A. Stothard F.S.A while copying these figures, fell from a ladder and was killed; his remains were interred in the churchyard immediately below the window:... "* Charles Stothard

was a leading authority on such things, having been the author of *Monumental Effigies*. St Andrew's contains the oldest stained glass windows in Devon, that is outside of Exeter Cathedral.

The church was the first of two in Devon, the other being Haccombe near Newton Abbot, to have the status of becoming, in 1333, an arch-presbytery. William de Ferrers, who was responsible for the building of the church, must have done some sort of favour for the king in order to establish this arch-presbytery, which was like a small version of a monastery. The arch-priest had four priests in his charge, each of the four having his own altar for services. In the sixteenth century the south aisle was added, making room for yet another altar. Their cell was opposite the church, the priests living a peaceful existence in this glorious location.

Alas, in 1979 this church was declared beyond repair, but that didn't wear well with the locals. A concerted fund-raising effort, involving a great majority of the villagers, and the financial help of English Heritage, enabled some £80,000 to be raised to ensure that this church did not become redundant or ruined.

The Tamar Valley branch line crosses the mouth of the Tavy at its confluence with the Tamar, before detouring slightly inland to reach Bere Ferrers. The line, which provides a truly beautiful ride into those parts of the valley 'that other cars fail to reach', is well worth trying for anyone who hasn't yet done so.

A terrible tragedy befell Bere Ferrers station in 1917 when a misunderstanding led to the deaths of ten men, their ages ranging from 20 to 40 years. A contingent of troops from New Zealand were travelling from Plymouth's former Friary Station to Exeter and beyond to Salisbury Plain in an eighteen-carriage train. They had not eaten since breakfast but had been told, when they left Plymouth between 3.00 p.m. and 3.30 p.m., that they would be fed at the first stop, this being Exeter. Two men in each carriage were detailed to fetch the rations from the guard's van at this stop. However the train made an unscheduled stop at Bere Ferrers and the New Zealanders, probably unaware of the geography of the county, may well have thought that they were in Exeter. The train was far too long to fit this small country station so many of the coaches were beyond the platform. However, this would have been somewhat irrelevant because the ten men, who were just seconds away from a gruesome death, had believed that the side from which they had entered the train was the one on which they should exit it when stopping. It's thought that they had been told to wait for a further order before getting off but this had been ignored. Coming in the opposite direction, from Exeter, was an express train which approached Bere Ferrers at a modest 35 miles per hour, but the station is on a bend and there was no way the engine driver, J. Skinner of Exeter, could have stopped even if he had seen the men. The driver of the troop train was unaware that anyone had alighted. It was the fireman on the Plymouth-bound train, Charles Henry Thorn, who shouted, "Whoa, soldiers on the road!" but this was to no avail as the train driver applied all the brakes, pulling up some 300 yards along the line before returning to see the awful scenes of carnage on and beside the line. There were some 'lucky ones' who either hadn't got off or had jumped clear. The inquest jury passed a verdict of 'Accidental Death', no blame being apportioned to either the trains' personnel or the railway company because the signals clearly warned of an approaching train. There is a memorial, in Bere Ferrers church, to the ten New Zealanders who perished in that terrible First World War accident. Over the years relations and friends of the victims have been back to see where their loved ones were killed. The memorial was re-dedicated in August 1989 in the presence of Bryce Harland, New Zealand's High Commissioner.

The signal box at Bere Ferrers Station, standing beside the platform, is not all what it appears to be, for it is one which was brought here, by road, from my home 'village', Pinhoe on the edge of Exeter, and to see it given a good home is a personal pleasure.

Bere Ferrers is located on a spit of land referred to in Saxon times as Birland, a *bir* in old Irish is 'a point' and in Welsh 'a spit', both appropriate as this small place is on the tip of a peninsula twixt the Tamar and Tavy. It has also had other variations in its name, Beer Ferris, Beer Ferrers or just plain 'Beer town' being in common usage in Victorian times.

The church of St Andrew is beside the Tavy and a stone's throw away from it is a riverside pub where I will always have fond memories of sitting outside on a fine summer's Sunday eating the 'freebies' on offer. Most pubs, these days, do nothing, some run to peanuts

to make the punters thirsty, others provide small chunks of cheese but this one excelled itself by handing over a basket of some of the best roast potatoes I have ever sampled!

And, of course, there are those who came to this place before me in those days when the Tamar saw a veritable fleet of paddle steamers plying between Plymouth and the great number of small ports of call along the way, Bere Ferrers being one of them. In 1860 the enterprising Mr Jackson set about catering for this influx of

river travellers. His tea gardens were the talk of Plymouth, a mouth-watering treat to anticipate on the northward river voyage; home-grown Tamar fruit, depending on the particular season, the richest clotted cream and gallons of tea awaited the visitors. He even set up a large marquee so that revellers could dance off some calories before rejoining their vessel.

For many years there was a regular ferry crossing place here to Blaxton (or Blackstone) on the east bank, the first mention of it occurring in 1263. Ordnance Survey maps show Blaxton Quay at the mouth of the short Blaxton Creek. Occasionally sheep were ferried over the river here and if they became a bit 'uppity' the ferryman, or the accompanying shepherd, would splash water into their faces, this having the desired affect of calming them down.

Ashleigh Barton, a short way inland from Blaxton, is a reputedly haunted house where a long-established floating phantom has appeared in upstairs rooms to warn residents of an imminent death in the family.

When the railway line, to Tavistock and beyond, was built there were various natural obstacles in the way, this wide mouth of the Tavy being just one of them. To bridge the gap a viaduct, comprising eight bow-spring girders, had to be cleverly constructed. This was not a simple job for the estuarine mud, which had accumulated over the years, had reached a depth of about 80 feet and as a solid rock anchor was essential, much skill had to be employed in creating the necessary foundations. The workers, or navvies, were treated to an unusual form of accommodation when working on this viaduct. HMS *Bittern* had been rendered redundant but, before finally being scrapped, she was to serve one more useful purpose. She was bought 'for a song', by the railway contractors, and then adapted for floating accommodation with the installation of more than a hundred bunks, this work being done in the dockyard at Devonport. When ready she was taken to a mooring at the mouth of the Tavy, close to the site of the viaduct which was about to be built over the following two years in the late 1880s.

Beside the viaduct, 'Tavy Bridge', there used to be the busy wharf of Yellowstone Quay. Being on the Tamar side of the rail bridge it continued to see trade after the arrival of the railway, many bargees preferring to unload here rather than having to lower and then raise masts to pass under the 'new' obstruction. Cargoes which passed through this quay included yet more of the delightful 'Dock dung', grain, timber and farm produce. The hinterland of this quay was a very productive one in its heyday. River barges remained a frequent sight on the Tavy until the early 1920s.

The Tavy and Tamar waters mingle in glorious surroundings off Warleigh Point where Tamerton Lake also seeks to join them. A 'No Through Road', Station Road, runs from Tamerton Foliot, along its creek, to the former railway station, which served the village. Beyond the railway a footpath leads into the woods and nature reserve at Warleigh Point. For anyone who likes great scenery this is a lovely and atmospheric place to explore and provides the best vantage point to see where the Tamar and Tavy rivers unite.

Rachel Evans saw this corner of Devon in mid-Victorian times and had this to write about it: "*A stranger remaining in the neighbourhood ... would do well to extend his rambles to the romantic little village of Tamerton ... supposed to be the Tamare of the Romans; and with it the appearance of notability. It stands on a small creek formed by the river Tavy. There are deep woods and rising hills around; and above all is seen the bold outline of Warleigh Tor. Tradition still points to 'the fatal Oak' on the village green, known by the name of the Copplestone Oak, as the living witness of a dark murder; pity it is that so fair a tree should bear so foul a stigma; blasted in appearance as in fame, it stands the warfare of time, a sad emblem of the undying records of crime. The legend of the oak forms the ground work of Mrs Bray's novel of Warleigh; it has been ingeniously woven into a tale of fiction, on the authority of some papers said to have been found at the family's mansion, as well as on that of old John Prince, who states that it 'cost Copplestone thirteen good manors in Cornwall, to buy out his pardon for the murder of his godson'.*" Apparently John Copplestone was angered by the boy's resentment of his strong and foul language and killed the lad as he left the church.

Warleigh, on the banks of the Tavy's estuary, has been home to many of those who are laid to rest at this church. It was built in the twelfth century and enlarged three centuries later. It is rumoured to be haunted by the ghost of Edgar the Peaceful, who obviously didn't quite live up to his name. He, too, was a murderer, his victim being Ethelwald, husband of Elfrida, who he slew in the park, on the slopes rising above the Tavy.

And on that 'happy' note our energetic river mingles its waters with the Tamar, our journey having run its course from the mist-shrouded moorlands to the more benign lowlands. We have seen tragedies, rain (and lots of it!), fled floods, carried coffins, deposited dock dung and dwelled on disputes, mentioned mines and murders and almost sat on an Elephant's Nest! It is hoped that you enjoyed this armchair journey *Along The Tavy*, enough to try the other two books in this trilogy, *Around & About Tavistock* and *Around & About Roborough Down*.